Andy and Annie

Eggert Thomsen

Andy and Annie
Copyright © 2020 by Eggert Thomsen

ISBN-13: Paperback: 978-1-64749-184-0
         epub: 978-1-64749-185-7

All rights reserved. No part of this publication may be reproduced, distributed, or transmitted in any form or by any means, including photocopying, recording, or other electronic or mechanical methods, without the prior written permission of the publisher or author, except in the case of brief quotations embodied in critical reviews and certain other noncommercial uses permitted by copyright law.

Although every precaution has been taken to verify the accuracy of the information contained herein, the author and publisher assume no responsibility for any errors or omissions.No liability is assumed for damages that may result from the use of information contained within.

Printed in the United States of America

GoToPublish LLC
1-888-337-1724
www.gotopublish.com
info@gotopublish.com

Andy and Annie

After a day of shopping and doing a few chores around the house, my wife and I felt kind of tired so we went to bed early. Louise and I have been married for nearly 60 years. We have six children who have long since been married and have families of their own. The grandchildren are our pride and joy. Louise dotes over them and keeps track of all their accomplishments. We both feel that we have been blessed and have had so many good years together.

I woke in the middle of the night to find my wife sitting on the edge of the bed. "What's the matter Louise"? "Can't you sleep"? I asked. "No Andy, I have terrible pains in my lower back". "Can I get something for you", I asked. "No Andy, I will be alright'. The pain persisted and she finally let me get some aspirin for her",

"Louise, I think you had better see the Dr." She replied in an annoying tone, "I will go to the Dr. When I am ready". Louise had always been very strong minded and I had long since learned not to question her decisions. As time went on, she became more irritable and I suspected that she was in the early stages of Alzheimer's disease. This was very hurting and difficult to accept since we had had so many good years together. At times, she would get almost mean and was after me almost constantly, It seemed that I couldn't do anything right. This is typical of Alzheimer's sufferers to be the most mean to those closest to them. I bore the brunt of this, saying nothing to anyone. 'They never suspected because when we were with the rest of the family, she was very pleasant, even to me, but as we got in the car to go home, it was back to the meanness.

Louise's pain became quite severe and unbearable. She finally agreed to see the Dr. and was given several tests. The Dr.

decided to send her to a specialist who had his practice in a larger city which was about an hour and a half's drive from our home. After examining her, they set up an appointment to have a biopsy taken from her pancreas and liver. Two days later, the Dr. called and asked that we come to his office for a consultation. We went into his office and the Dr. said, "Please sit down. I am afraid I have some rather bad news for you". "Louise you have pancreatic cancer that has spread into your liver". "The prognosis is that you have about six months to live". Louise and I looked at each other. The tears began to run down my cheeks. I was devastated. Louise came over to me and said, "whatever it is it is'. "We still have six months together".

"That's right", the Dr. said. "We will do everything we can to treat this". I told the Dr. that I had tried to get Louise to go to the Dr. sooner. He said, "IT wouldn't have made any difference". I asked the Dr. "where do we go from here"? He replied, "We will begin chemotherapy right away and also give her some oral medications". We left the doctor's office, which was in the cancer center, and started the drive home. For several miles we sat there in silence. I looked over at Louise and saw a tear run down her cheek. I reached over and took her hand. She looked over at me and said, "it's all right. We'll fight this thing together". As we were driving, Louise said," you know any problems that families have, disagreements, or petty differences become irrelevant". "Our being together, our loving God and family are what is important'. I said to Louise, "it's too bad that it takes something like this to put things into perspective". "Louise, I will always be at your side loving you and caring for you". As the days went on, Louise became more difficult to be around. No matter what I did it was wrong. Between that and the staggering medical bills, it became almost unbearable.

I suspected that Louise was in the early stages of Alzheimer's. As the days went on, she became more difficult to be around.

For a long time I bore the brunt of it saying nothing to anyone. 'Then one day after one of her tirades, feeling hurt and very downhearted I finally went to my daughter's house to talk to her about the situation. She said, "I knew something was wrong but didn't know if 1 should say anything". She also said, "If things get too bad come over here". So when things got too tough I would go to my daughter's house and talk to her and her husband. This would case the hurt. 'The daughter's husband and | had always been close friends. I| could not think more of him than if he had been my own son. I will always be so thankful to my daughter and her husband for their caring and support during those trying times. As Louise's treatment continued, the tests and x-rays were not encouraging. 'The cancer continued to spread and her pain became increasingly severe. Her condition worsened, in spite of all the medications and chemo treatments. Then one day she turned a yellow color. I called the Dr. and he said to bring her to the hospital right away. The Dr. examined her and admitted her. He took me aside and said, "She will never go home again". They put her on a morphine pump so that she could self-administer her pain medication.

One day she said to me, "we need to talk". She smiled at me and looked into my eyes and said, "I will soon be gone". "Afterwards, I want you to go forward with your life." "Don't mourn for me too long". "You have a lot of life left". "I want you to promise me that you live it to the fullest". We both had tears in our eyes and I said, "Yes honey". "I promise you that I will". She also asked that I look after her older brother. He is a bachelor living alone. I promised that I would occasionally drive the 200 miles to visit him.

Louise's condition worsened. They put her in a hospice facility where they really took good care of her and did everything possible to make her comfortable. | stayed there in the room with her. 'They had a bed for me, lounging for people that came

to visit her, a refrigerator and other amenities. I stayed there day and night with her. It was so hurting and difficult to see her go down Hill a little bit every day.

'The day before she passed away, being barely able to speak, she turned to me and said very faintly, "I love you". She kissed me and closed her eyes. 'Those were the last words she spoke. 'The next day as I was holding her hand, she peacefully passed away.

All of our children, some of the grandchildren, doctors, nurses, cleaning ladies and friends were all in the room with her. Almost everyone in the room had tears and was crying even the Dr. They had all grown to love Louise during her short stay in the hospital. It was so hurting to see her go but it also was a relief to know that she was no longer in pain.

We had services in the church with a viewing. During the services, I was surrounded by our children, grandchildren, many relatives and friends. After the services, she was taken to be cremated which was her wish. The next day the family gathered at the Cemetery for her in inurnment.

After the services, I went home to the older two story house that had been our home for nearly 50 years and was so full of fun and laughter. Suddenly, it was very quiet and lonely. It was difficult to sleep. So many memories would creep into my mind. I lay there and would think about the happy times and also the troubling times in raising a family. 'Times were sometimes financially tough, but I guess those times were also happy even though we were struggling.

'The ensuing days were extremely difficult, such an emotional strain. I cried many times each day. Being home alone after our nearly 60 years together seemed almost unbearable. Seeing her picture and so many of her things would bring back memories

and there were tears again. I would open the closet doors and see her clothes hanging there. I put my arms around them and held them close to me and the tears would stream down my cheeks. It was a very hurting time. My family was very comforting, especially my daughter that lived close. She and her husband would invite me over to eat with them. I will be forever grateful to them for their help through these trying times.

It seemed that life was very stressful. I had an appointment with our family Dr. for a regular checkup. He would say to me, "hey man, how are you doing"? I told him about the stress and he said," go for a walk every day, this is a great way to relieve stress". I took his advice and began walking every day. I was not working at this time. I had taken time off from my part time job to be with Louise through her illness. So, every day I walked regardless of the weather. Part of my route would take me to the Cemetery. While there, I talked to Louise and God. I would say," Hi Louise", "I love you and miss you". I would also talk to her about things at home and happenings with the family. I then told her," well I'm going home". "I love you". I would then finish my walk, occasionally my daughter and her husband would walk with me.

I went to church every Sunday, usually with my daughter and son-in-law. They were always so good to me, which helped tremendously. My two sons called me quite often which also was very comforting.

In going through some of Louise's things, I came across a poem she had left for me. The poem said," Look up at the moon and the stars, you will see me smiling down at you with all my love". 'This was very touching and at the same time made me happy. I knew then that she loved me. I also had the feeling that it was time to get back to my life.

I went to a nearby town and applied for a part time job with a telemarketing company. Things went very well for me there, and I found that I had a good telephone voice and good rapport with the people I contacted. Soon I was making a very high percentage of sales and commissions. It seemed that the rewards were almost routine. It felt good to receive the MVP certificate and I began to enjoy things again.

Church was very comforting to me and the people were very kind. They were all my friends. I continued walking every day and was slowly getting back to my normal self, which was to be a "happy go lucky" type of person.

On a very beautiful spring morning, I went to church and was sitting there alone in my usual seat. Annie Hollison came up to me and said," Hi Andy". I looked up and said," Hi Annie, how are you this morning"? Annie said, "I have a question for you Andy". I see that you walk every day, would you care if I walked with you"? I said, "Annie it would be just great to have somebody to walk with and I sure would welcome your company". Annie said, "thank you Andy, call me when you want to walk". Annie was a widow lady. She had lost her husband 11 years ago. She was very attractive and I had known her most of my life. In fact, some of her children had attended school together with mine. Her oldest daughter and my oldest daughter were good friends and were in the same class in school. My oldest son was also in the same class as Annie's son. Annie has neuropathy in her feet and legs. The Dr. told her that walking was very good therapy.

After going home from church and it was such a beautiful day. I decided to call Annie to see if she wanted to walk with me. She said, "sure Andy this is a wonderful day for a wall". We decided to meet about half way between our homes. We lived about eight blocks apart. We met at our designated meeting place and began our wall. It was a little awkward at first but having known

each other most of our lives we soon began talking and it seemed that we had so many things to talk about, her family and mine. It made walking together a lot of fun we both looked forward to the next day. The 3 miles we walked every day seemed to go by so quickly.

One of the subjects we talked about was the loss of her oldest son. He was killed in an auto accident, only 16 years old. He was a very promising musician. He and four other boys had formed a rock 'n roll band. 'They played for dances all over the area. They were on their way to play for a dance when the Van they were driving blew a tire and rolled over into the ditch. Her son was thrown from the van. It rolled over on him causing severe injuries. He was taken to a nearby hospital, bur the injuries were so severe that he passed away the next day. Their band was becoming quite prominent. They even opened the show for "Sonny and Cher". A nationally known husband and wife musical team. His band has since been inducted into the "rock and roll" Hall of Fame. 'The loss of her son is a hurt that Annie carries with her always. His funeral services were held in the school auditorium because of the large crowd that attended. Andy knows that losing a child is the most hurting.

About 30 years after losing her son, Annie's husband was diagnosed with lung cancer. They had been married for nearly 50 years. He was treated in the same cancer center where my wife was treated. 'They made many trips there to receive chemotherapy and all the treatments involved in trying to cure his cancer. Annie took care of him at home, doing everything she could for him for nine months. She said it was very hard to see him going down Hill every day. The hospice people were notified and were beginning to set up things for his comfort, but he passed away before this could be arranged. Two days before he passed away, he took Annie's hand, held it close to him and kissed her hand. 'The next morning he went into a coma and

never came out of it. He passed away the next day. All of Annie's family, the minister and his wife, neighbors and the Dr. and his wife, that were good friends, were all there when he passed away late that afternoon.

There were some very lonely times after her husband's passing. She kept busy baby sitting with her grandkids. As they grew older, new babies were born, keeping her busy. They all love their grandma and even now they keep in close touch with her. Being a widow for 11 years and in all those years, before she and I got together, she never dated. This was puzzling to me because she is such a good, wonderful person.

Her other son lives on a farm acreage a few miles from town. He and Annie and a grandson raised ostriches there. Annie spent a lot of time on the acreage helping with all the work connected with that operation. After a few years they quit raising the ostriches, because there wasn't a close enough market for them.

Every day, after I got off work, I would call Annie and say, "hi Annie". "I'm home". "Shall we walk today'? Annie said, "Sure, I have been waiting for you to call", We met in our usual place and began our 3 miles walk. We both know so many of the same people and it was always so much fun to stop and talk with them. Annie is 78 years old, and I am 80 and it seemed that the 3 miles we walked every day would go so fast. We would walk every day, talking about our families and our lives. It seemed that we were never at a loss for words. Neither Annie nor I had any intentions of ever entering into another relationship, but it seemed that she and I were so happy when we were together. Our walk would end at the intersection near her home. She would go into her home and I continued walking to my home. While walking home alone, I would think to myself that Annie and I were beginning to get close. She would call me every morning before I went to work. My thoughts were, "Annie is

such a wonderful person and thoughts of her were ever present in my mind. I would call Annie every night before I went to bed.

As we were walking one day, I reached over and took hold of Annie's hand. She pulled away and I was embarrassed. We walked a little farther and she said," I just didn't want anybody to see us". "Iris a little soon after losing your wife and your family may not understand". I thought for a minute and I said to Annie," I don't care if they see us". "I care for you very much". Annie answered, "and I care for you". We continued our wall holding hands.

When we got to Annie's home she said, "I baked some cookies". "Come in and I will give some of them to you". I said, "I'll just wait at the door". She went in and got the cookies. She gave some of them to me. I thanked her and walked the eight blocks home thinking "what a wonderful person she is". The cookies, by the way, were very good. We talked over the phone again that evening.

Annie and I sometimes go to a nearby city that is situated by a large lake. One of the parks has a sidewall that goes around it and is about a mile in distance. It is a beautiful setting and Annie and I would sometimes walk around it two or three times. There were ducks, geese and boats on the lake. Some were fishing boats and the others were pleasure boats.

We are so happy together, always laughing and joking and having such a good time. Some of the townspeople remarked that Annie and I were walking together. "Oh, they are just friends". Someone else remarked, "but they are holding hands". They are all so happy for both of us. It is still a mystery to me that someone had never tried to date Annie. They sure, "missed the boat". There just isn't a nicer person.

Sometimes when walking, Annie and I walk into the Cemetery. We stop at her husbands and sons graves and say a prayer. We then go to the other side of the Cemetery where my wife is buried. We always say a short prayer and Annie says, "we love you Louise".

While walking, we sometimes take a different route that would lead us to a bench on the main Street of our little town. We would sit there for a few minutes, talking and usually had a laugh or two people began to call this our "love bench". Some more of our happiness.

We were walking one day and a person that knows both of us very well came over to us and said, "I have seen you guys walking together and it brought to mind a song that fits well" the name of it is, "the second time around". He also said, "we are all happy for both of you".

While walking toward home, I said to Annie, "I love you Annie". She quickly responded, "I love you too Andy". We opened our hearts to each other while walking. We have no secrets and are openly honest with each other and so much in love.

That evening Annie and I were talking over the phone and I asked, "would you like have dinner with me"? "Yes, I would like that', Annie said. So we set a date and both looked forward to it. However, early in the afternoon before the date, Annie called and said, "I can't go with you tonight because a friend of mine that is ill with cancer is having a birthday party". "I just can't turn her down'. "I hope you understand". I said to her, "oh sure Annie", "I do understand". "We will make or another time". "I worked every day. Annie and I walked I got home and later talked on the phone. A few days later, I asked her again if she wanted to go to dinner with me. With her big smile, she said to me," of course Andy". "I was afraid you wouldn't ask me

again". On the way to the restaurant we were like a couple of kids on a first date. We sat across from each other at the table. We looked at each other and both laughed. After all the walking and talking, we didn't know what to say to each other. We soon loosened up and were back talking and doing our usual talking and laughing. I could just feel the love and happiness between us. It was a feeling of wanting to be together forever.

Each day, I just couldn't wait to see Annie. I would meet her at the halfway point and when she came into sight, I had that happy feeling just to see her. As we walked, Annie said, "I baked some more cookies and when we get to my place I'll give you a bag to take home". We arrived at her house and she said, "come in and I'll get the cookies for you". We went into the kitchen; I took the cookies and gave her a hug. She hugged me back. This was the first time we had ever embraced. I thanked her for the cookies and started to leave, but when I got to the door, I turned and came back to her. I said to Annie, "just one more thing". I took her in my arms and we kissed. I felt her arms around me and we just held each other. I said to her, "I love you Annie", to which she replied, "I love you too Andy". I left with my bag of cookies and walked toward home with a feeling of elation. Annie told me later that she watched me walk away toward home and she said to herself, "he likes me, he likes me'. She also told me that she had a tear of happiness. The following Sunday in church, I surprised Annie. She was sitting in her regular seat and I walked over to her and asked, "care if I sit with you"? She looked at me, rather surprised, and said, "sure sit down Andy". She had wondered what the reaction might be from the congregation, but I think we pleasantly surprised them and they were glad for both of us. Annie, of course, is loved by everyone. Her happy personality, along with her kind, caring feeling toward everyone just seems to male them all love her.

Andy and Annie

The church has a very special meaning to both of us. 'This is where Annie and I first got together. We both feel that God put us together there. Our congregation is small and they are all our friends closeness not found in most churches. Our pastor, a very kind and considerate person, is a friend to all of us. Annie's children and mine went to Sunday school there and were confirmed there. Some of them were also married there.

Annie and I talked about getting together, but it was less than a year after my wife's passing. Although we cared so much for each other, Annie thought it might be too soon and this may hurt my family. We both decided that I should talk to the pastor and get his advice and thoughts regarding our situation. After hearing our concerns, he smiled and said, "you Andy, faithfully lived up to your vows and took care of Louise to the end". "Now it is time for you to move ahead with your life". He also said, "I thought maybe there was something between you and Annie having seen you in church together". "Now Annie, the pastor said, "you took care of your husband, faithfully being with him and caring for him until he passed away". "As I told Andy, it is also your turn to move on with your life". We told the pastor that neither Annie nor I had any intentions of ever getting married again but our feelings toward each other just seemed to happen. The pastor said, "I'm sure that God put you two together". "You have our blessings". Kiddingly, he added, "you can even hold hands in church". Little did he know, we were way ahead of him and had been holding hands all along? I told the pastor that we were not yet to the marrying stage. He said, "I am here when you need me". "God bless both of you".

We did our usual walling every day and were so very happy together. By that time, I was visiting Annie in her home in the evening. We watched TV together and sometimes we just held each other. It was very tempting to spend the night but Annie said, "I am just as temped as you are Andy but to the

community that would make our relationship look cheap". "We are so close with the congregation that we just cant do that". Annie, of course, was right, but I did say to her, "I want to marry you Annie". She looked at me for a moment and said, "I want to marry you too, but we will figure that out later".

Annie asked me, "do you like to dance"? "Sure", I replied, "but about all I can do is a slow waltz". She said, "I'll teach you to rock 'n roll". We went to the basement in her home, which had a lot of room. We found some rock 'n roll music on the radio and Annie proceeded to teach me to dance. We even did some jitter bugging later. It was so much fun that we decided to go dancing where an area band was playing. A couple of the musicians in the band were Annie's cousins. We got so that we danced pretty well together and we went almost every weekend to where the group was playing. We became friends with several of the people that also loved to dance. There was very little drinking, maybe a beer or two. They were a very nice group of people and a lot of fun to be with.

While talking with Annie, she told me that sometimes during the 11 years that she was alone, she would get quite lonesome. She told me about standing in the kitchen, and asking God to please send someone to love her. Annie said, "he really answered my prayers by putting you and me together". "Andy, you are so good to me, caring, kind and loving". "Thank you God",

One evening, I decided to walk to Annie's house for a short visit. We sat on the couch. We calked, had our usual laughs and watched TV for a while. Suddenly we woke up. It was 2:30 in the morning. We jumped up. Annie said. "what shall we do"? "What will the neighbors think"? We decided that Annie should take me home. We went to the garage to get her car. On the way out | stumbled after tripping on a large flowerpot that I didn't see in the darkness. We opened the garage door very quietly. Annie

backed out of the garage as quietly as possible. We did not turn on the lights and drove very slowly to the corner. Alter turning the corner, Annie turned the lights on and drove to my home. Later, we laughed and Annie asked, "do you really think that we fooled anyone"? It took a while for the bump on my leg to heal.

We were sitting in the living room one evening and I asked Annie, "will you marry me"? Instantly Annie replied," of course I will Andy". "I love you so very much". So appropriately, I got down on one knee and asked her again. I said to Annie, "I love you with all my heart".

We discussed the possible dates and decided to get married in about a month. We told our families and went to their homes to break the news to them. My family was very surprised and we got mixed reactions, from very happy for us to reserved emotions. I think they were taken by surprise. Annie's families, on the other hand were elated and so happy for both of us.

Annie and I decided that we wanted a simple wedding, nothing elaborate. We wanted anyone that wanted to come to our wedding, to come as you are, no gifts and everyone was invited. We did not send out any invitations, but just told everybody about the wedding and the date. It seemed that the word mushroomed and the night of the wedding the church was packed full. It was a fun affair, so much laughter and happiness. We decided not to pick anyone to stand up with us so that we would not slight anyone in either family. So during the ceremony, the pastor said that anyone that wanted to stand up with us could come up near the altar behind us. To our surprise about half the people came and stood up with us. A gesture that Annie and I will never forget. We had a reception in the church basement afterward. It was a lot of fun, lots of laughter. Many of the people stood up to wish us happiness. The reception was nothing elaborate, just cake and coffee, punch, sandwiches, potato salad and other salads.

So, Annie and I were off to a new adventure as we went forward with our lives together. We decided to live in Annie's home. My recently divorced daughter and her two grown children moved into my house, which was a timely situation for them.

The one hurt in our wedding was that two of my daughters did not come to the wedding ceremony. We thought it was probably difficult for them to see their father marrying someone else. But we learned that that was not the case at all. The day of the wedding my daughter's husband was diagnosed with terminal cancer. My other daughter stayed with them to give them support and comfort.

My family has grown to love Annie and they know how much we mean to each other. This has made Annie very happy. She had worried that she had caused a split in our family. It is not in her nature to hurt anyone. We both love our families, both sides very much. Annie's family has also been very good to me.

My sons send flowers to Annie on mother's day. They tell her chat they love her and sometimes call her mom. This is not in deference to their mother, just the fact that they do care for Annie. Annie says, "I'm not trying to take your mothers place". "I care about all of you and I dearly love your dad".

The day after Annie and I were married, we went to a dirt track racing event in a nearby city. My grandson and my granddaughters' husband drove racecars at that track. They raced in what is called the modified class. It is usually the largest class that races on the dirt tracks. The public announcer said, "Andy Martin is in the crowd today and he is celebrating his 81st birthday" the crowd cheered. 'Then the announcer said, "Oh by the way, he and Annie just got married last night". We got an even bigger ovation. I suspect that my daughter had tipped him off.

We love to dance and do so whenever we can, however, the second year we were together Annie began having trouble with her right knee. She subsequently had a total knee replacement. This is a very painful procedure. but Annie with her grit and determination toughed it out and was soon walking normally again. She religiously did her therapy, it healed well and we were soon able to do our walking and dancing again.

I left the telemarketing job I had and took a part time job with a large grocery chain. Shortly after, Annie also got a part time job there. We both enjoyed that very much. We became friends with most of the employees and also with many of the customers. Annie and I have been together for about five years now, Our day begins with a hug, a kiss and an "I love you'. After saying our prayers at night, the day ends with a hug, a kiss and an, "I love you". There have never been two people that were meant for each other more than Annie and L. It is a happiness that is difficult to describe.

Annie's left knee, which has been bothering her for some time, finally got to the point where she had to have knee replacement surgery. After surgery, she went through rehab again and it turned out very well. In fact we were soon back to our dancing. She went back to her job at the grocery store only four weeks after the surgery. The surgeon that did both of her knees, has become a friend and he calls Annie "sweetheart."

Annie and I decided to visit my daughter's husband who was very ill with cancer. He always had liked Annie and when we walked into the room, he said, "Annie, I am in trouble". The minister was also there. My daughter had to go into town to take care of some business, so Annie and I and the minister stayed with her husband. He was so dependent on my daughter that he wanted her to be with him every minute. While she was gone to town he tried to call her on the cell phone, but couldn't

reach her and he became quite agitated. A few minutes later. He passed away, but before he passed, he said, "You know you can't die without living and you can live without dying". Those were the last words he spoke and he passed away before my daughter returned home from town. He was a religious man and we know that he is now with God.

I care so much for Annie that every once in a while I say, "thank you God for Annie'. Then I say, Thank You God for Annie. We sometimes wake up in the night and just lay there talking, sometimes about family, the weather, our church or what we plan to do the next day or we just lay there holding hands and even occasionally, we sing together. Our life is just being together, full of love and happiness.

We enjoy going to church so very much and we especially like to hear two ladies, one playing the organ and the other playing the piano. They play together and it is so very beautiful.

Almost every Sunday after church, we visit the nursing home here in our small town. There are about 10 people that we visit there and it gives you such a good feeling to see their faces light up and to see their smiles when they see us. God bless them. When we leave the nursing home, they ask us to please come back but don't wait so long the next time. We leave there feeling how lucky we are to be together and to be in our own home.

Annie keeps track of all the birthdays and anniversaries for both her family and mine. This is no easy chore. I have 19 grandchildren, 18 great-grandchildren, along with my six grown sons and daughters and their husbands and wives. Annie has a son and a daughter, nine grandkids, 12 great grandkids, plus many relatives and friends. Obviously, it is quite a chore to keep up with all of them, but she does religiously.

Annie's grandson introduced us to a very well-known person that does musical concerts all over the nation. He also performs in England, Europe, Africa and almost anywhere in the world. In addition to that, he has his own television show that is rated number one in its category. He also has appeared in several movies and is an accomplished actor. We have become good friends with him and know him to be a super good person. Annie and I went to one of his concerts. We went into the concert hall where he was rehearsing. When we walked in the door, he was up on the stage, but when he saw Annie and me, he came right down to us and gave us a big hug. We occasionally talk with him over the phone.

Annie and I visited my son in Michigan. On the way there we crossed Lake Michigan on the ferry. The ferry is actually a huge ship and also carries semi tractors and trailers many cars motorhomes and so forth. It takes about four hours to cross the lake and it is quite a fun trip. We went up on the top deck toward the front of the ship. Suddenly, they blew the big horn. It is very loud. We almost jumped out of our skin. But then we had a good laugh. My son lives just a few miles from where the ferry docks. We spent a couple of days visiting with him and his wife. From there we drove to Ohio to attend Annie's grandson's wedding reception. We enjoyed dancing and visiting with the families.

My grandson is getting married in Colorado in June. We will also attend that. I also have a granddaughter that is getting married in the fall. Annie and I will dance "up a storm" at both of those weddings. Our families keep us very busy, but we enjoy every minute of it.

When Annie and I both pass away, there would be nothing to show our life and love together. We both are to be cremated and buried with our first partners. So we have devised a plan. Annie's family is buried on the West side of the Cemetery. My

family is buried on the East side of the Cemetery. Annie and I have decided that we would put a small tombstone in the center of the Cemetery. The stone will be inscribed "Andy and Annie". So after we have passed away. We will leave it up to our sons and daughters to put a small portion of our ashes into a small urn and to bury them there by the stone.

As of this writing, Annie and I continue walking. holding hands, being with family and friends. We both love nature, including flowers, trees and gardening, birds and animals. We dance whenever we can and have so much fun meeting and talking with our friends and family.

We cannot leave out our pet, which is a large yellow tomcat. He weighs about 35 pounds, and usually meets us at the door when we come home. He is always close by wherever we are at home.

It is such a good feeling, that our families respect and love us and keep in touch with us. Both Annie and I lost our first partners and have felt despair and loss. It seemed that we would never be happy again but don't you believe that you cannot love again, because as God has shown us, there is "a second time around".

If you should ever be in the Cemetery in our small, quiet little town, and if you should see the small stone engraved, "Andy and Annie", this is the story behind that.

www.ingramcontent.com/pod-product-compliance
Lightning Source LLC
LaVergne TN
LVHW041552060526
838200LV00037B/1260